图书在版编目（CIP）数据

鱼类 /（英）哥瑞斯·琼斯著；苗萌译. —西安：世界图书出版西安有限公司，2018.1

（我的动物朋友）

ISBN 978-7-5192-3818-6

Ⅰ. ①鱼… Ⅱ. ①哥… ②苗… Ⅲ. ①鱼类—青少年读物 Ⅳ. ① Q959.4-49

中国版本图书馆 CIP 数据核字（2017）第 276385 号

First published in England in 2017 by Booklife Publishing.
Text and illustrations copyright © 2017 Booklife Publishing.
Bilingual: English-Simplified Chinese translation copyright © 2017 by World Publishing Xi'an Co. Ltd.
Bilingual: English-Simplified Chinese audio, video and APP copyright © 2017 by World Publishing Xi'an Co. Ltd.
All rights reserved.
本书仅限中国大陆地区发行销售。

书　　名	鱼类（我的动物朋友）
著　　者	[英] 哥瑞斯·琼斯
译　　者	苗　萌
策划编辑	陈宇彤
责任编辑	陈宇彤
装帧设计	诗风文化
出版发行	世界图书出版西安有限公司
地　　址	西安市北大街 85 号
邮　　编	710003
电　　话	029-87214941　87233647（市场营销部）
	029-87234767（总编室）
网　　址	http://www.wpcxa.com
邮　　箱	xast@wpcxa.com
经　　销	新华书店
印　　刷	鹤山雅图仕印刷有限公司
开　　本	787mm × 1092mm　1/12
印　　张	4
字　　数	20 千字
版　　次	2018 年 1 月第 1 版　2018 年 1 月第 1 次印刷
版权登记	25-2017-0059
国际书号	ISBN 978-7-5192-3818-6
定　　价	45.00 元

版权所有　翻印必究
（如有印装错误，请与出版社联系）

本书英文原版为英国国家图书馆馆藏图书。本书与英国、美国、加拿大三大英语系国家同步出版。

目录

第 4–5 页
什么是生物？

第 6–7 页
什么是鱼类？

第 8–9 页
它们的栖息地

第 10–11 页
鱼类的家园

第 12–13 页
它们的食性

第 14–15 页
它们如何呼吸？

第 16–17 页
它们如何行动？

第 18–19 页
它们如何生长？

第 20–21 页
神奇的鱼类

第 22–23 页
打破世界纪录的鱼类

什么是生物？

所有的生物都具有生长、发育、繁殖的能力。
生物需要空气、营养、水和阳光。

这些都是生物。

青蛙　　老虎　　人类

刀，叉，盘子。

书

这些都是非生物。

非生物不具有生长、发育、繁殖的能力。非生物不需要空气、营养、水或阳光，因为它们没有生命气息。

泰迪熊

什么是鱼类？

鱼类是生活在水中的生物。它们需要空气、食物、水和阳光才能生存。三文鱼、鳗鱼和鲨鱼，都属于鱼类。

三文鱼

鲨鱼

鳗鱼

鱼类是脊椎动物，通常都有鳍，用鳃呼吸。它们是冷血动物，它们的体温会随着外界温度的变化而变化。

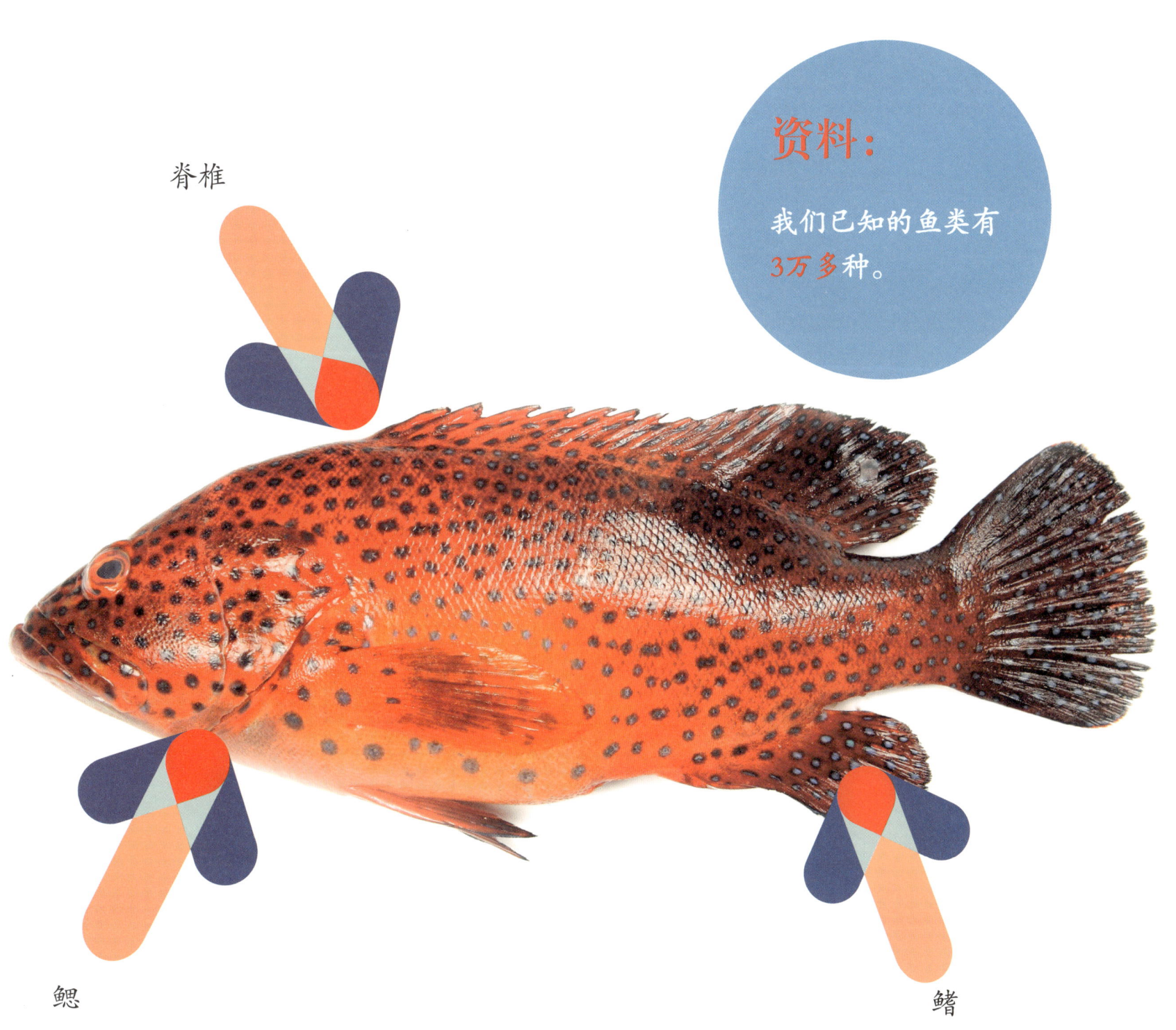

脊椎

鳃

鳍

资料：

我们已知的鱼类有 **3万多种**。

它们的栖息地

所有生物都有它们的栖息地或家园。鱼类生活在溪水、河流、池塘、湖泊或海洋中。

一些特殊的鱼类既能在水里呼吸，也能在陆地上呼吸，但是它们只能短暂地离开水源。

这种弹涂鱼（跳跳鱼）可以在陆地上呆三天之久。

鱼类 的家园

锯脂鲤（水虎鱼）生活在南美洲的河流里，它们以超锋利的牙齿而被人类熟知。

鱼类生活在世界各地不同的水域中。淡水水域是鱼类常见的栖息地。在水中能够躲避**捕食者**猎捕的地方很少，所以它们通常要将自己很好地**伪装**起来。

成千上万种鱼类生活在海洋中的珊瑚礁上。礁石为它们提供了躲避捕食者的避难所和藏身地,并帮助它们在捕食猎物时不被发现。

珊瑚礁

资料:
澳大利亚海岸边的大堡礁是世界上最大的珊瑚礁。

它们的 食性

资料：

众所周知，大白鲨曾经吃过鲸鱼。

大白鲨

鱼类以其他鱼类或植物为食，或是两者混食。以其他动物为食的鱼类，如大白鲨，被称为**食肉动物**。它们能借助超灵敏的嗅觉寻找5公里以外的猎物。

鱼类用嘴巴进食。一些鱼类具有锋利的牙齿，能够帮助它们将猎物撕成碎块。另一些鱼类则借助其上下颌骨磨碎食物。

锋利的牙齿

资料：

一条锯鳐一生当中牙齿数量可达17,000颗。

13

它们如何呼吸？

所有的鱼类通常通过头部两侧的鳃呼吸。它们通过鳃吞咽水，并将水中的氧气输送到身体的其余部分。

鱼鳃

14

有些鱼,如弹涂鱼(跳跳鱼),也可以在陆地上呼吸。它们就像青蛙和蟾蜍那样通过皮肤呼吸。

它们如何 行动?

鱼的鳍帮助它们在水中自由穿梭。当尾鳍推动它们在水中移动时，其他的鳍则帮助它们保持平衡、静止和改变方向。

尾鳍

鳍

金枪鱼

有些鱼，如蝠鲼（魔鬼鱼），它们的鳍长在身体的两侧。它们用强壮的身体肌肉拍打鱼鳍。当它们游动时，看起来像在水中飞行。

蝠鲼（魔鬼鱼）

它们如何生长？

大部分的鱼是卵生动物。有时鱼爸爸们会照看他们的卵或带着他们的卵，直到小鱼**孵化**。

雄性海马随身携带一个装有卵的特殊育儿袋。

小鱼孵化后,它们的爸爸妈妈不再照看它们。它们需要自己寻找住所和食物。

神奇的鱼类

河豚为了保护自己免受捕食者的侵害，它们会将身体膨胀变成球。锋利的刺布满全身，让捕食者望而却步。

双髻鲨鱼（锤头鲨）长着奇怪的扁平锤形头。它们的眼睛长在头的两侧，方便它们随时随地发现猎物。

眼睛

打破世界纪录的鱼类

鲸鲨

资料： 鲸鲨比两辆公交车放在一起还长！

纪录： 世界上最大的鱼

尺寸： 身体长达 19 米

旗 鱼

速度： 高达每小时110公里

纪录： 世界上速度最快的鱼

资料： 旗鱼游泳的速度比狮子奔跑的速度还要快。

23

FISH

Grace Jones

ANIMAL KINGDOM

世界图书出版公司
西安 北京 上海 广州

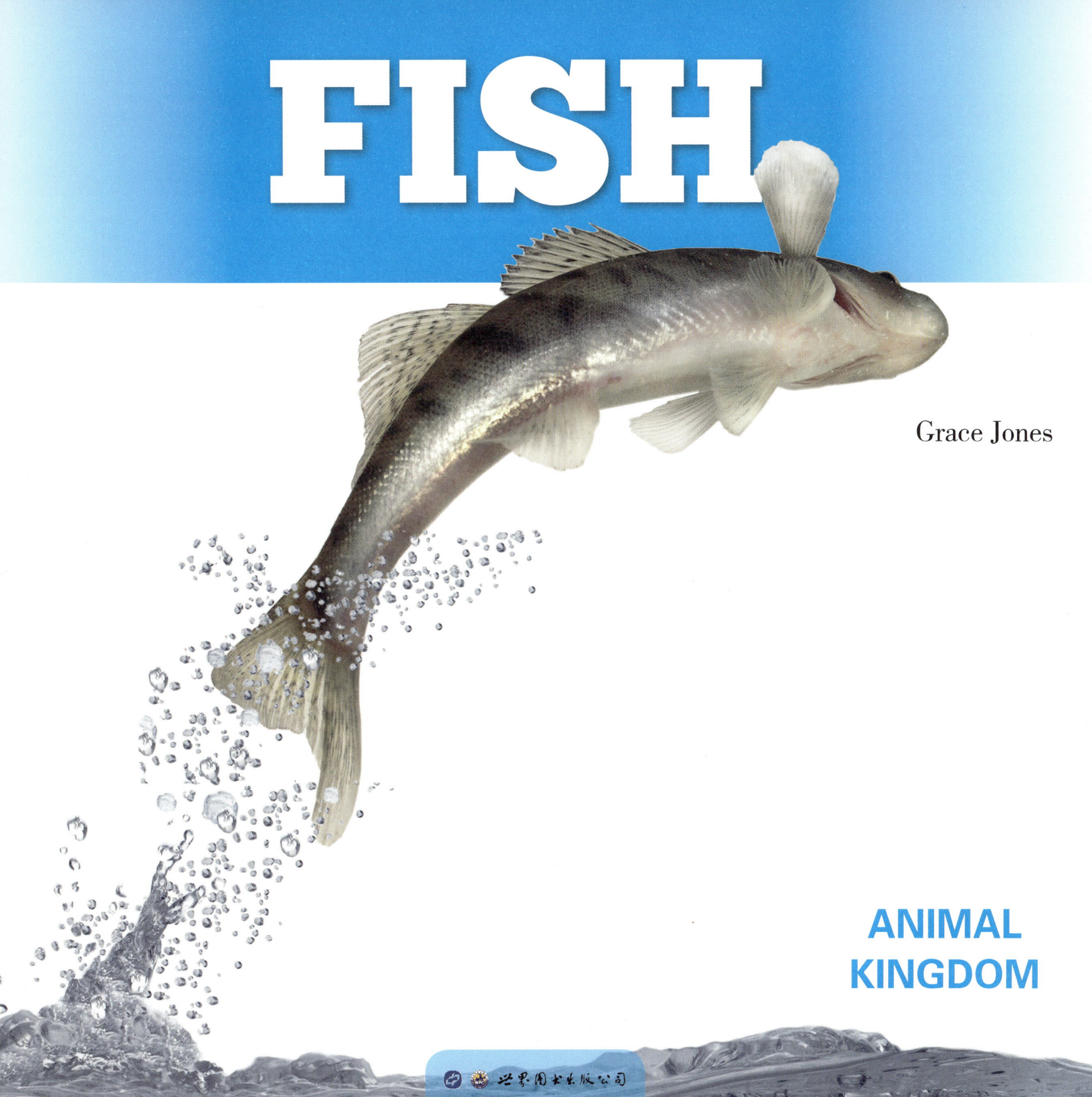

Words that appear like **this** can be found in the glossary on page 24.

contents

Pages 4-5
What Are Living Things?

Pages 6-7
What Is A Fish?

Pages 8-9
Where Do They Live?

Pages 10-11
Fish Homes

Pages 12-13
What Do They Eat?

Pages 14-15
How Do They Breathe?

Pages 16-17
How Do They Move?

Pages 18-19
How Do They Grow?

Pages 20-21
Fantastic Fish

Pages 22-23
World Record Breakers

Page 24
Glossary & Index

A catalogue record for this book is available from the British Library.

What Are Living Things?

All living things have the ability to grow, develop and reproduce. Living things need air, nutrition, water and sunlight to stay alive.

These are all living things.

Frog

Tiger

Human

Knife, fork & plate.

Books

These are all non-living things.

Non-living things do not have the ability to grow, develop and reproduce. Non-living things do not need air, nutrition, water or sunlight because they are not alive.

Teddy Bear

5

What Is a Fish?

Fish are living things that live in water. They need air, food, water and sunlight to live. Salmon, eels and sharks are all types of fish.

Salmon

Shark

Eel

Fish usually have fins, breathe using gills and have a backbone. They are also cold-blooded animals. This means that their body temperature changes when the temperature outside is hotter or colder.

Fact: There are over 30,000 known species of fish.

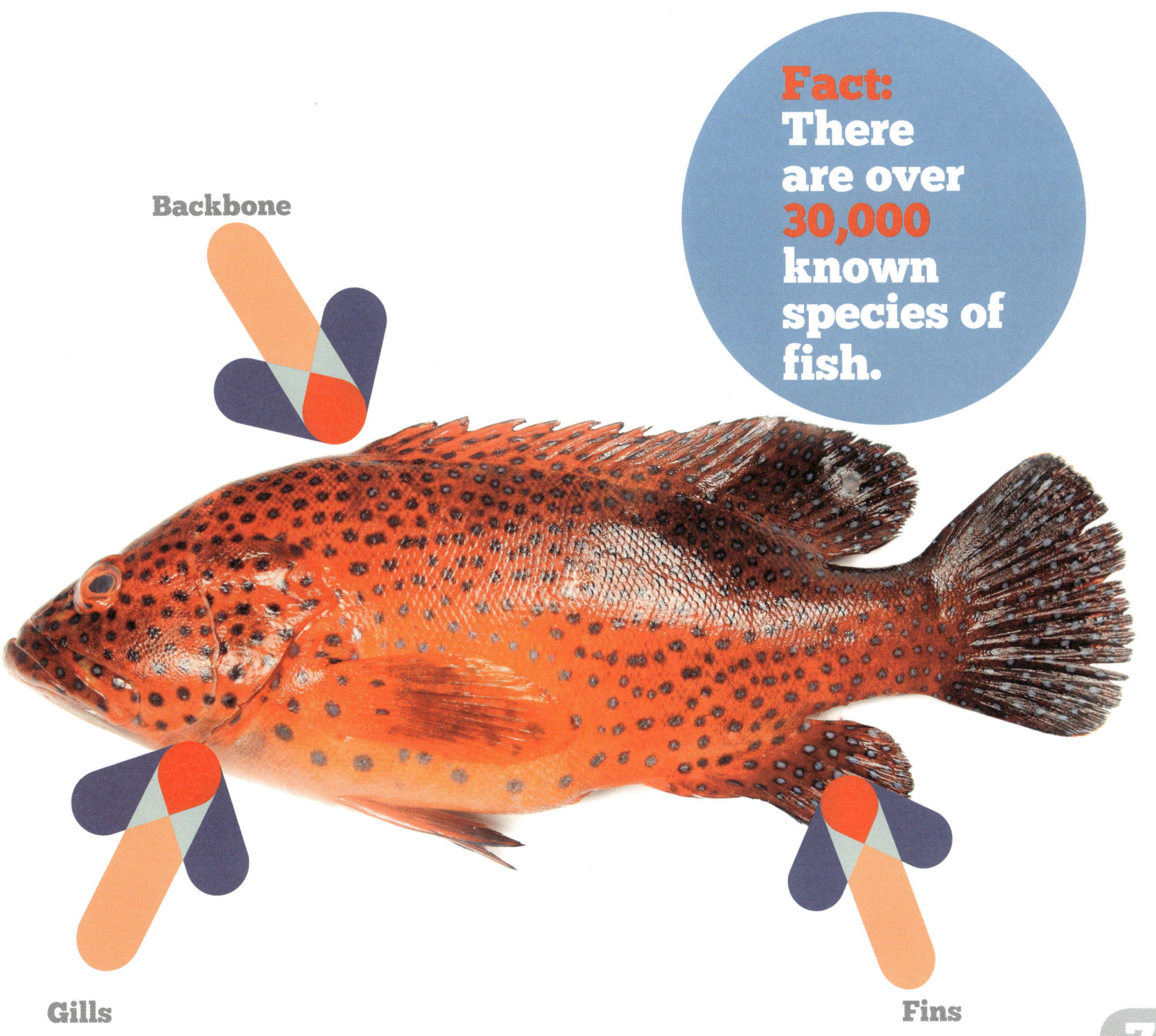

Backbone

Gills

Fins

Where Do They Live?

All living things live in a **habitat** or home. Fish live in streams, rivers, ponds, lakes or oceans.

Some special fish can breathe in the water and on land. Although, they can only leave the water for a short amount of time.

This Mudskipper fish can live on land for up to three days.

Fish Homes

Piranhas live in the rivers of South America and are known for their super sharp teeth.

Fish live in many different underwater habitats around the world. A common habitat for fish are fresh water rivers. There are fewer places for them to hide from predators in a river so they are usually well camouflaged.

Thousands of species of fish live in the ocean on coral reefs. The reefs provide them with shelter from predators and places to hide so they can catch their prey without being seen.

Fact: The Great Barrier reef off the coast of Australia is the largest coral reef in the world.

Coral Reef

What Do They Eat?

Fact: Great White sharks have been known to eat whales before.

A Great White shark.

Fish eat other fish or plants, or a mixture of both. Fish that eat other animals, like the Great White shark, are called carnivores. They use their super sense of smell to hunt out their prey from over three miles away.

12

Fish eat using their mouths. Some have very sharp teeth to help them tear their prey into smaller pieces. Others grind their food in-between their top and bottom jaw.

Sharp Teeth

Fact: A **Sawfish** can grow up to **17,000** teeth in their lifetime.

13

How Do They Breathe?

All fish breathe through their gills which are usually on either side of their head. They swallow water through their gills and oxygen in the water moves throughout the rest of their body.

Gills

Some fish, like the Mudskipper fish, can breathe on land too. They often breathe through their skin just like frogs and toads do.

How Do They Move?

Tail Fin

Fins

Fish have fins to help them swim through the water. Their tail fin pushes them through the water, while their other fins help them to balance, stop and change direction.

A tuna fish.

Some fish, like manta rays, have their fins at the side of their bodies. They use their strong body muscles to flap their fins. When they move, they look like they are flying in the water.

Manta Ray

How Do They Grow?

Most fish start life as eggs. Sometimes fish fathers look after their eggs or carry them until they hatch.

Male seahorses carry their eggs around with them in a special pouch.

18

After they hatch, their parents do not look after them. They look for shelter and food to eat on their own.

19

Fantastic Fish

Puffer fish protect themselves from predators by puffing up their bodies into a ball. Sharp spikes appear all over their bodies so predators do not try to eat them.

Hammerhead sharks have strange flat, hammer shaped heads. Their eyes are on each side of their head so they can see their prey wherever they are.

Eyes

World Record Breakers

WHALE SHARK

Fact: The Whale shark is longer than two buses put together!

Record: The World's Biggest Fish

Size: Up to 19 metres long

SAILFISH

Speed: Up to 110 kilometres per hour

Record: The World's Fastest Fish

Fact: The Sailfish swims much faster than a lion can run.

23

Glossary

Camouflaged: when an animal is hard to see because they are the same colour as their habitat.

Carnivores: animals that eat other animals rather than plants.

Habitat: a home where animals and plants live.

Hatch: when a baby animal or insect comes out of its egg.

Predators: any animal that eats other animals and insects.

Prey: any animal or insect that is eaten by another.

Index

Breathe 9, 14, 15

Fins 7, 16, 17

Food 6, 19

Gills 7, 14

Grow 4, 5, 18

Home 8, 10

Living Things 4, 5, 6, 8

Move 16, 17

Water 4, 5, 6, 14, 16, 17

Photo Credits

Photocredits: Abbreviations: l–left, r–right, b–bottom, t–top, c–centre, m–middle. All images are courtesy of Shutterstock.com.
Front Cover – Levent Konuk. 1, 24 – Krasowit. 2–3 – David Mckee. 4bl – Chros. 4c – Eric Isselee. 4r – michaeljung. 5bl – Elena Schweitzer. 5tl – koosen. 5r – Lichtmeister. 6bl – Alexius Sutandio. 6br – bluehand. 6tr – UnderTheSea. 7 – wanchai. 8 – Krzysztof Odziomek. 9 – Super Prin. 10 – aastock. 11 – Brian Kinney. 12 – withGod. 13 – Natursports. 14 – jirawatfoto. 15 – sunsetman. 16 – holbox. 17, 22 – magnusdeepbelow. 18 – LauraD. 19 – Hans Gert Broeder. 20 – Beth Swanson. 21 – Matt9122. 23 – stockphoto mania. 25 – Willyam Bradberry.

ANIMAL KINGDOM

What is a living thing? Where do animals live? What do animals eat? How do they move and grow? Learn the answers to these questions in this exciting new series. With easy to read text and informative diagrams, this series offers a simple introduction to the animals that live in our world.

FISH

REPTILES

AMPHIBIANS

BIRDS

MAMMALS

INSECTS